I0149167

All Scripture references taken from the KJV
of the Holy Bible, unless otherwise indicated.

Sift You Like Wheat

by Dr. Marlene Miles

Freshwater Press 2023

ISBN: 979-8-218-12972-9

Table of Contents

Sift You Like Wheat 5

God Lays Claim, Satan Lays Claim 8

Working *for* the Devil? 16

God Speak 20

You Are the Giant 22

Stealing Virtues 27

A Nation Inside of You 30

Scattered Nations 32

Scattered *Among* Nations 34

The Sifting 39

Tossed 43

Captivity 45

Evil Pastors 52

You, Yourself 57

When Anything Goes, Anything Comes 63

Humpty Dumpty 65

My Pit 69

Pull Yourself Together 72

Military Weapon 75

But I Have Prayed for You 81

Been Sifted 84

What Is Old Age? 91

Re-Membered: Put Back Together 94

Dear Reader 96

Other books by this author 97

Who remembered us in our low estate:
For his mercy endureth for ever:

And hath redeemed us from our enemies:
For his mercy endureth for ever.

Who giveth food to all flesh:
For his mercy endureth for ever.

O give thanks unto the God of heaven:
For his mercy endureth for ever.

(Psalm 136:23-26)

Sift You
Like Wheat

Most assuredly, you will need the
Holy Spirit for this book.

Freshwater

Freshwater Press

Sift You Like Wheat

Jesus said to Peter, **"Satan has *asked* to sift you like wheat."**

Satan asked whom?

GOD.

How?

Evil Petition, most likely.

When?

24/7

Where?

Throne of Grace, and or other *Thrones* of Heaven.

No matter how we look at this, we must acknowledge that Jesus knows what Satan has asked God. Is it because in the presence of God when Jesus was in Heaven, He historically heard Satan accuse the brethren and ask to *sift* them? Or is Jesus speaking of something that recently happened and He is extemporaneously reporting it to Peter?

And the Lord said, Simon, Simon, behold, Satan hath desired to have you, that he may sift you as wheat: (Luke 22:31 NKJV).

We look at various translations of the same passage of Scripture. In one we see that the devil has **demanded** permission to sift you like wheat.

Did Jesus mean Peter, and Peter only, or Peter only of the Disciples? Did Jesus mean Peter and all of the Disciples? Or does this desire to sift even apply to *everyone— even us*? Even now? And how does the devil get to **demand** such?

Another version says Satan has *asked* to sift each of you like wheat (BLB).

Simon, Simon, behold, Satan demanded to have all of you to sift like wheat, (KJV).

Simon, Simon, Satan has asked to sift all of
you as wheat. But I have prayed for
you, Simon, that your faith may not fail.
And when you have turned back,
strengthen your brothers."

But he replied, "Lord, I am ready to go with
you to prison and to death."

Jesus answered, "I tell you, Peter, before
the rooster crows today, you will deny
three times that you know me."

(Luke 22:31-34)

Satan has asked to *have* you; he
boldly asked God.

God Lays Claim, Satan Lays Claim

Satan lays claim to mankind --, as many as he can, from birth. Some, he lays claim to *before* birth. It all depends on what your ancestors did, agreed to, and traded as part of whatever they got from idol *gods*, false *gods*, demons, or Satan himself. They could have made a deal with the devil or the dark kingdom knowingly or unknowingly. Anytime a demon or other dark entity believes that it has proffered a service to you, then a deal has been struck and you owe them. They unrelentingly believe you owe them worship, you owe them payment of some kind, and that payment can be your children. Owing your first born is not just an old wives' tale, it is a demonic demand from dark kingdoms.

Therefore, if your ancestors made devil deals of any kind, **you** could already have been claimed by the devil **_before_** your birth.

By what means did this happen? It could have been through witchcraft, divination, that your ancestors may have participated in knowingly or unknowingly. It could be from any other initiation or deal they may have brokered with the evil one.

The devil can be successful against many who do not know the Lord, are not saved, do not know the Word of God, even though they may be saved and profess Christ. And he may be successful against those who are saved who do nothing, even if they know the Word of God. If they are dry, living a prayerless and careless life, planning salvation as their burial insurance only, and not walking in salvation while they live, they can be defeated in this life, *and* the life to come.

Just as Satan was at the Throne of God discussing Job, it is along those lines for other humans. As it pertained to Job, Satan kept going back to ask for more latitude to do horrible things to Job. If Job had done as his wife, and misguided friends advised, he would have been and remained defeated in this life and if he had cursed God, he would have gone to Hell, and therefore defeated in all eternity. In that case, Satan's claim to Job would have been successful against Job.

Satan claimed Esau.

God claimed Jacob. He said, *Jacob I have loved; Esau I have hated.* Also, we read in Psalms, *While you were yet in your mother's womb, I knew you.* God already knows who we are and who we are destined to be, from the beginning; we don't surprise Him. We all have a relationship with God, He knows us, He claims us, or He doesn't. He draws us. He saves us. He loves us. We want to be claimed by God.

Before I formed thee in the belly I knew thee; and before thou camest forth out of

the womb I sanctified thee, and I
ordained thee a prophet unto the nations,
(Jeremiah 1:5)

We must do something about the one
that claims us, if it is **not** the one that we want
to be claimed by. Some people love evil;
some are naturally good. Those who love evil
and cursings will gravitate to that and may
want to be claimed by the devil. This is not a
game where we are picking a team for
dodgeball. This is real life, and eternity.
Those who are naturally good will reject the
devil instinctively--,we hope.

Esau *accepted* Satan's claim and
ended up serving Baal.

Jacob accepted God's claim, thereby
rejecting the devil's claim, which is pretty
much default on Earth. Jacob ended up being
an ancestor of Jesus Christ.

Does the devil really have *authority*
to do this *sifting*? He goes up to the Throne
of God to accuse mankind because of man's
sin. He seeks and gets authority to do this by

judgements from evil petition. He gets license by ancestral iniquity. He gets open doors and inroads by evil covenants, and evil initiations. Sin is the fire starter, always.

The devil continues to do things that he has done against you and your family before you were saved, unless and until you make demands and decrees that he **stop**. If you don't, often he won't. That's what all this praying is about. At times he also does things by outright illegal activities that if you don't notice or don't do anything about it, he just runs roughshod.

My book, **<u>Evil Petition</u>** goes into how the devil tries to get a Throne judgement against a man. If he gets that judgment, then he has a right to *sift one like wheat*. Accusations in Heavenly Courts are made 24/7 by the Accuser of the Brethren. That book discusses how to handle oneself in the Courts of Heaven. Also, in that and most of my books there are prayers and warfare prayers to pray your way out of spiritual trouble.

IYKYK. If you know, you know. If you know what your authority is in Christ, you will stand in it and assert your spiritual rights in spiritual matters. If you know the Word of God and have read the Bible to the end, you find out that we have already won in Christ Jesus, and ultimately in the end we win. If you know who you are then you know that you must assert your authority, or you will be run over. You are or should be a threat to the kingdom of darkness and that is why you are--, why mankind is under attack.

That goes as in life. If you are the boss on your job, then you boss, if not those who should be your subordinates will run amok and all over you. If you don't know you're the boss, but they do, they are often threatened by you, or may be jealous of you and your authority. This happens even if you are trying to be *friends* with them. IYKYK.

As a parent, if you don't assert certain authority in your household, your kids will run all over you--, especially if you are trying to be **friends** with them. IYKYK.

But it takes more than just knowing, you must also take action and be diligent. When you are in your proper place and walking in God-given authority, in Christ, you are the boss of so many evil entities, and the devil hates that, violently.

Those who do wickedly against the covenant he shall corrupt with flattery; but the people who know their God shall be strong, and carry out great exploits, (Daniel 11:32).

What *exploits*?

Those exploits are doing spiritual things; and therein is the beauty of this. We are in a flesh body; we look like just regular people. We all know that most who are in flesh are tempted to be *only* in flesh, and never rising any higher. The devil wants to inundate our flesh senses to make us think or believe that we are *only* flesh.

But we are multi-dimensional beings, able to and expected to move in multiple dimensions. So, when we, in our flesh bodies, also do great spiritual works, that is a marvel sometimes to us. Those marvelous spiritual things that we can do through Christ are the *exploits*.

Those exploits are also a marvel to the unsaved Seeker. Exploits are powerful witnessing tools; it's why they are given, for the benefit of all, to further God's plan in the Earth, and to win others to the Kingdom.

It is also to show, help, and heal those who are still only flesh sighted and flesh minded who may already be saved but may need to rededicate their lives to God for a deeper walk with Christ. Deliverance is one such exploit.

Jesus came to Earth enrobed in flesh. *Why?* To do certain **spiritual** work in the Earth that could only be done in a flesh body.

Insert your name here: _____ came to Earth, enrobed in flesh---, why? To do certain **spiritual** work in the Earth that can only be done while having a flesh body.

Jesus did His work in three years. What will your story be? While we don't rush our natural lives, what will your story be for the 100 years or so that you are *here--, a spiritual being, in flesh*?

Working *for* the Devil?

Most of the people that I have encountered who have a violent reaction to the Name of Jesus, someone speaking the name, Jesus--, the Bible, the Gospel, the Good News or any type of evangelism are often already *claimed* by the devil, and he has installed, and they have accepted anti-Christian entities in their souls that **manifest** at any of the above. Those people have been *claimed*. It doesn't mean that they can't get out of the devil's clutches, but the claim is deep-seated and may be long running in their bloodline.

Is the devil sifting those who belong to him? Maybe, maybe not. As long as he has you in his grip, things may go along okay, because he knows your eternal destination is NOT with God and it is with him. Can you imagine a person's life going along okay and then at the end they get the surprise of all surprises--, they've been serving the devil all along, and they end up in Hell?

What value are you to him in Hell? Is it just to torment, torture, and hate you? Well, he'd get the pleasure of knowing that one of God's creations lost their soul and he has it.

The devil could be getting work out of you now, while you're on Earth. Did you know you can be working for the devil in your life and not even be aware of it? *Monitoring spirits* comes to mind. Some humans are *monitoring spirits*. Personally, I suspect drama queens and drama kings, folks who like to keep something going as well as gossips and blabber mouths to be human *monitoring spirits*. Or it could be the person who says next to nothing, but their eyes and/or ears are always alert and on a certain someone that they work with, socialize with, arc related to, or certain strangers they see on the train on the morning commute. Those people could be working for the devil, unawares.

How?

They are signifying, nosey, always looking into other people's business, or obsessed with one person alone. They may or may not be a gossip, but often they are. At night when asleep, people can receive and answer evil summons. While asleep, your spirit/soul can be summoned to a witchcraft coven or other place. There, you can be prompted to spill all the tea, and tell everything you know about so and so. Wake up in the morning and never know you did or said anything--, the dream could be totally wiped. Get ready, go to work, or wherever, and there, again, gather as much information as you can about the object of your assignment.

Did you see her today? What was she wearing? How about her hair? And those shoes. She ate lunch with Bobby today. What do you think is going on with those two?

Do you know you are working for the *devil*? Nope. You don't know anything and would never believe it if somebody told you.

But if you are on assignment for the devil, you have been *claimed* and you appear to be agreeing with the claim. Well, you don't seem to be disagreeing with the claim.

I'm telling you.

To the positive and the negative we are surrounded by a great cloud of witnesses, (Hebrews 12:1).

God Speak

You will need the Holy Spirit for this book; it is for those with *ears* to hear.

In the same way Jesus spoke in Parables, God speaks in a way that He is saying something more and something deeper than just the words in the Bible--, the words on the page. that's why the Bible is deep and understanding it takes not only lifetimes, but it also takes the Holy Spirit. The Holy Spirit has eons and millennia of experience--, an infinite amount of Knowledge, Wisdom, and Understanding. Without a thousand or even 100,000 Words He can impart to those whom He inhabits, and those who listen to Him vast amounts of spiritual awareness, knowledge, Wisdom and power. These are instant downloads. Actually, He can do it *faster than instantly--*, with a quickness that is unknown to the flesh and unknowable to the human mind. It just *is*. Human words in any language are often not sufficient to communicate **Spirit**, even though the Words that Jesus speaks are Spirit and they are Life.

There is so much more.

Therefore, many times, when man thinks that God is talking about something in the natural, God is really talking about something in the Spirit--, something more, something deeper and more impactful.

Yes, He is talking about something in the physical, but that is not all there is. Because God is Spirit, He also speaks in and out of *Time*, which is a full dimension unto itself. If you can understand Spirit and Time, you are that much closer to understanding God.

You Are the Giant

Whose fan *is* in his hand, and he will
throughly purge his floor, and gather his
wheat into the garner; but he will burn up
the chaff with unquenchable fire,
(Matthew 3:12)

Satan has desired, asked, demanded, asked permission to *sift* you like wheat. While we may think this is a physical request, it is a **spiritual** request. Note, Jesus said, *Like* wheat.

Sifting, as in wheat is separating the wheat from the chaff.

What is chaff?

It is the husks of corn or other seeds. If you have ever juiced veggies, all the peelings that are left over and good for compost or are not consumed; is as chaff. Of course, that is where most of the fiber is, but in this parable, the chaff is not usually of value or desired. Chaff is separated from the wheat by winnowing or threshing, separating it from the husks, hulls, bran, pods, shells, sheaths, or shucks.

As this parable is about people, the chaff are those who are not saved, do not want to be saved, enjoy evil, and will always follow evil. Those may be the folks that the devil laid claim to, and they accepted the evil claim, or did not reject the demonic claim on their life. They will become chaff and will be burned up with an unquenchable fire.

When separating wheat from chaff, or chaff from the wheat, what blows off because of winnowing or is forced off by threshing is considered as worthless as rocks when one is panning for gold. The wheat is the *gold*.

Threshing is separating what is useful from what is not useful. Wheat makes flour. Couscous is wheat, semolina is wheat. Bulgar is cracked wheat. Farina is finely ground wheat, often cooked up as breakfast porridge. Farro, spelt, durum, emmer, and graham are other versions of wheat or flours with varying coarseness and uses. Wheatberries are the whole kernel of wheat and include the bran.

Wheat feeds people. It nurtures them. It provides nutrition and sustenance and makes them able to grow, to thrive. While we all need some roughage in our diets, there are certain shells and husks that we don't eat.

Of course, the devil wants to take what is useful and leave you what is not useful for your life and your godliness, because he does not want you to have any godliness. He doesn't want you to use God-given gifts, talents, abilities, or virtues to serve God. He wants you broke so you have no means to worship the Lord in tithes and offerings.

Really, he wants full control of you, to even dismantle you to see what you're made of. He wants to shake you, shake your faith; he wants to take your faith, if possible and leave you with the trauma of the shaking. He wants to leave you with all that is not faith, doubt, unbelief, and suspicion of God.

The devil does this by trauma and sudden terror, sudden destruction, abuse, and chronic abuses in life. In this way, the sifting is violent. It can be obviously agitating, painful--, or the devil is subtle; some have been sifted and never knew it. How can that be? Some of this sifting can happen at night while we are asleep. If our dreams are wiped or ignored, not properly interpreted, we may never know the real consequences of sex in the dream, eating in the dream or other things that happen to us in the dream.

I've met people like that--, people who want to *sift*. You may have as well. Perhaps they are on assignment from the evil one and may not even know it. Some know it. They behave as though they want to see what makes you tick, what makes you work. Some want to take you apart like they are engineering students and you're a lab project. Don't let them do that. If you come across people like that, keep them out of your purpose and business. Don't give away the plans for your life that God has given you.

Stay prayed up and ask God what and how much to share with people that you see or suspect are there to dismantle what you are doing, or even take you apart.

As you become more aware of who you are and walk in your authority, you may come to know *who* is trying to take you down, in the spirit – we do not war against flesh and blood--, but in the spirit. We also don't run to people and accuse them of being a witch, even if we know it's them.

Who is trying to take you down is doing so because you are supposed to be ruling over them, or taking authority over the powers that are inspiring and animating them. You are the Giant--, or you should be and will be when you rise up--, but you may think they are the giant in **_your_** life.

They do this in a number of ways. We will mention some of them, but who knows all the wiles of the devil, and who knows what new scheme he devised while I was typing this page? God. God knows. That's why we need the Holy Spirit every moment of our Christian life.

Stealing Virtues

Scattering our virtues, draining good things from us such as God-given gifts, talents and abilities is real. If we are not spiritually aware, spiritually sensitive, we won't even feel it or notice when it happens.

If your child needs an inoculation, haven't you seen the nurses try to distract the child while the injection is happening? Yeah, the devil does that to grown people. He gives us distractions—many times VERY pleasant distractions while he steals from folk. If that doesn't work, or in case he's tired of that method and wants to try something else --, he may use the trauma, sudden terror mode--, but it is still a distraction.

Jesus could feel when virtue was pulled out of Him. Jesus was focused and paying attention spiritually and wore the flesh life very loosely, so shouldn't we do that, too? If so, then we too would be able to detect spiritual things, even knowing when virtue is leaving us.

For an entire year I noticed that immediately after I prayed, I would get a phone call from individual. I believed this person to be a friend, but she was haphazard in that she really never wanted anything, and her phone conversations deteriorated to foolishness almost every call. After too many of these calls I saw the pattern. The prayers of the righteous availeth much POWER --, as soon as I had prayed, that person was on the phone, to drain the anointing. While I didn't want to be rude, I had to put a stop to it. People don't just waste your time if you let them, they will drain *virtue* from you. If not virtue, right after you pray you should be quiet, be still, and listen because that is a prime time for God to speak to you.

But this busy body whom I've named Megan is blowing up your phone, and you, by habit, answered it.

Hours go by...

Megan finally hung up the phone, and you are exhausted. You always are, every time the two of you speak or spend time together. Megan has pulled virtue from you. If you feel tired, weakened, drained, anxious, agitated, irritated or not yourself after dealing with someone or some situation— **virtue has been drained from you.** We call it a waste of time. In a sense time has been stolen, but virtue has been drained while they pick your brain or convolute your way of thinking as you try to answer their weird questions, for example.

Don't let that happen to you.

If you are not sure, or feel that nothing happened, nothing changed, pray, and ask God. Ask that He restore to you anything that was stolen in that exchange, in the Name of Jesus. Yes, we are to pour out to others, but you shouldn't feel used or drained every time. Therefore encourage one another and build each other up, (1 Thess 5:11).

A Nation Inside of You

Abraham, the Father of many nations, had *nations* inside of him, as do you. They are good *nations* if you are in Christ, and your generations remember the Lord.

And I will scatter you among the heathen, and will draw out a sword after you: and your land shall be desolate, and your cities waste, (Leviticus 26:33).

Throughout the Bible, God was ever warning His people to change their ways or there would be punishment. Even called of God you are not exempt from doing what He says do. We are born, we receive salvation, and we grow in the things of the Lord.

We do not despise small beginnings. Abraham was to be the Father of Many Nations, but he only had one child of promise, but he didn't even have that child until he was 100 years old. I would say that's a very small beginning.

We start small, so until you are a nation, you are a dwelling, then a city, then you grow. After you have given birth to children, either natural or raised spiritual children, you become a *nation*.

To the evil and to the negative the devil wants to scatter you, and the nation that you are to become, all over the place. Evil covenants, soul ties, bad relationships are some things that scatter people, and families. Disappointments and emotional upheavals can scatter people. As you are the nation or have a nation inside of you, if you are sifted, taken away by the wind and scattered, how will you minister to your generations? So, if you're the leader, the patriarch or the matriarch of a nation and the devil can strike and scatter you; he's taken down your generations; he's taken down a whole lot of people.

… I will smite the shepherd, and the sheep of the flock shall be scattered abroad, (Matthew 26:31b).

Scattered Nations

Thou didst march through the land in
indignation, thou didst thresh the
heathen in anger, (Habakkuk 3:12).

Do not forsake the *assembling* of
yourselves together – yeah, as a family, as a
group of like Believers, and you, yourself.

How can you assemble *yourself*
together? You can't really, but the following
are things you should do.

You do that by learning who you are.
That is discovered by learning who you are
to God, and who you are in Christ. If there
are no spiritual people to speak into your life,
and even if there are, just ask God, *Who am
I? Who am I to You? What is my purpose for
being on* Earth? What are my spiritual gifts
and assignments? Ask God everything and

anything, He will answer you. God always answers. It is incumbent upon you to know His voice. Sit still, be still long enough to hear His voice. After that, be obedient.

You begin the process of finding out who you are to God also by gaining knowledge, and truth. With study. With the Word of God –, find yourself in the Bible.

All of the above is deliverance. We can be delivered daily. Deliverance is not always instant; sometimes it comes in stages and is evidenced in how we change and grow spiritually, and sometimes that is daily.

If we fall under judgement with God, then the devil will certainly have his way to sift and scatter. When we receive deliverance that reverses and also prevents the sifting and scattering. Practicing the disciplines of the faith, we affirm who we are in Christ--, our identity and maintain wholeness. This is why we seek truth, knowledge, the presence of God and deliverance often, to maintain our souls and our being, so that we are not scattered.

Scattered *Among* Nations

I will scatter them also among the heathen,
   whom neither they or their fathers have
known; and I will send a sword after them,
till I have consumed them, (Jeremiah 9:16).

And the LORD shall scatter you among the
nations, and ye shall be left few in number
among the heathen, whither the Lord shall
   lead you, (Deuteronomy 4:27).

In some places in the Bible where it
says that God did, or will do a particular evil
thing, often it means that the Lord will **allow**
that thing to happen to the sinner, rather than
disallow it. Some of these things that we read
or see as evil (and they are not good), are
built into the Law of Sin & Death. Sin, the
great fire starter, is the reason the devil is
accusing mankind day and night. Sin is the

fuel that can make evil petitions burn against mankind.

Yet, we are careful not to blame God for things that God didn't do, especially things that are built into the Law. So if we sin, then the iniquity that follows--, it is what it is, if we do not repent and ask forgiveness and for Mercy. In that case God didn't do anything to us, the Law was already established; if we make the wrong choice, and do not repent, we get the bad results.

If you go out in a rainstorm you get wet. *God* didn't get you soaked; you chose to go out into the rain. Wet is built in to rain; you made a choice.

Blasphemy is blaming God for evil that God did not do. As well, Blasphemy is giving other than God credit, praise, worship for the good things that God did. God says that He will not give His praise to idols.

So, the devil captures a person (their soul) and begins to do whatever he wants to do to them, indoctrinate them, force them to do things against God because *idol gods, false gods*, devils, want worship. They want other things, but worship is what they want the most.

> And the Lord shall scatter thee among all people, from one end of the earth even unto the other; and there thou shalt serve other gods, which neither thou nor thy fathers have known, even wood and stone, (Deuteronomy 28:64).

> For the LORD shall smite Israel, as a reed is shaken in the water, and he shall root up Israel out of this good land, which he gave to their fathers, and shall scatter them beyond the river, because they have made their groves, provoking the LORD to anger, (1 Kings 14:15).

God is not evil, but if there is a judgment connected to sin, disobedience, rebellion, unbelief--- then that unrepented of sin brings the sinner under judgment. Under this judgment, there is Satan who wants to do stuff to humans, such as sift them like wheat, for example. Under Satan are demons that he uses to enforce judgments *after* he gets permissions that he gets to sift, toss, punish humans for their sins. Look how easy this is for Satan – sin has punishment, and without the Holy Spirit it is impossible to keep the commandments. Without repentance and the Blood of Jesus how will one escape the iniquity and the punishment of having sinned?

No, I'm not saying that the devil works for God. I am saying that the devil is the prince of this world and that he wants to do evil to people anyway. Without God's **protection** evil would be sitting at our door every day, all day, and every night, all night. Earth would be hell. But it is not hell, it is Earth, and thank God for that.

Repentance is protection. Salvation is protection. The Blood of Jesus is protection. God graciously, like a good Father offers His children many different forms of protection. So, when God's hands of protection are off of people, the devil gets to do what he wants to do to folks.

Now, to help you sin and make wrong choices, the devil sends in demons to infiltrate your soul, your thoughts, your decision making, and your will. You want to fast, but you end up not fasting. Yeah, you don't want to eat that cheesecake, but you end up eating it. You want to remain cool and not get angry, but you get angry and sin in your anger. Open door – more demons.

Wrong and stupid ideas such as being proud of how long you can hold a grudge. Unforgiveness. You'd better forgive; unforgiveness is too powerful of a weapon to put in the devil's hands. Do not by your own actions, help form weapons for the devil to use against you.

I will scatter them as with an
east wind before the enemy; I will
shew them the back, and not the face, in
the day of their calamity, (Jeremiah 18:17)

We all want and need God's face to us, not His back. Repent for the sins of your ancestors and repent quickly for your own sins so God's face will be toward you, and His protection will be afforded to you.

The Sifting

Sifting wheat in Bible times is not as we know as sifting today. In our times we may think of sifting through rocks for gold or sifting through a jewelry box for your grandmother's heart locket. Sifting flour as in baking. As said, sifting in Bible terms is separating wheat from chaff; it is *involved*.

Wheat is the grain that is grown to make flour or other products, such as bulgar, or couscous, depending on how it is ground. Sifting in the Biblical sense is really threshing, hitting that wheat so hard, shaking, or brandishing it, so that the chaff is separated from it, and only wheat remains. Threshing is pounding it against a rock, or a hard flat surface called a threshing floor to separate the useful part of the wheat from the chaff which is of no use at all.

The devil wants to sift us all, like wheat. Of note, God threatened Israel over and over and over again that He would separate them, scatter them, ... because of their sin, because of their idolatry. God said, **I shall be their God and they shall be My people**. That's basically the deal and can mankind just do *that*? Scattered means there is no protection, collectively or individually for the sinner that is under judgement.

Peter's faith was already on rocky soil, else Jesus wouldn't have said, **Peter before the rooster crows you will deny me three times**. Peter is about to go through and in going through some shaking, in that dark night, Jesus is saying that Peter will fail. Three times.

That's scary, because from dark until the rooster crows most of us are asleep. What are we doing in our sleep? Are we walking upright before the Lord as we do when we are awake? Or, are we somewhere in the spirit doing things that would make us not even recognize *ourselves*? As stated before, some sifting can happen at night while we are asleep, such as sex in the dream. According to Minister Joshua Orekhie, sex in the dream can lead to sickness, poverty and making a connection with the devil, among other things. This is all under the Curse of the Law, is it not?

In the world, three strikes would make us OUT. In the criminal justice system, three strikes takes a man out of society and puts him in prison. But there is no condemnation in Christ, even though that rooster crowing marked that morning after the night when three times, Peter had denied even knowing Jesus. If someone did that to us, even once, we'd be **done** with them.

Why didn't you introduce me to your friends? Didn't you see me standing there and you didn't introduce me? You didn't introduce me as your girlfriend--, I'm just Megan, just Megan? I'm just a friend and we've been dating for 2 years? Yeah, we'd be done if someone denied knowing us or acknowledged our relationship with them.

Every morning there are tender mercies, and that may be because from dark to dawn, when that rooster is announcing the sun's rising, have we been, like Peter, *denying* the Son of God? Or have we been doing as Peter believed he would, following

Jesus everywhere, to prison or to death, but that was while Peter stood before the Lord, wide awake. What are we doing at night before the rooster crows? People, this is all your life, every night for 100 or so years!

But Lord, let us pray anyway and repent for the things we know not of, that we may have done. Amen.

Tossed

Sifted, scattered, tossed--, when God's hand of protection is off you, this is what will happen because the devil is hell bent on doing this to man. Agitate, irritate, shake, toss about, disturb, cause to wander.

The devil doesn't personally do this tossing and sifting. PEOPLE will do this to those who will be sifted. The person, their mind, their faith, their soul, their emotions, can be mishandled in so many wrong relationships or situations. Their soul and spirit can be tossed about by winds of doctrine. People whom we do not war against, in the flesh, are employed by Satan to do things to other people.

That we henceforth be no more children, tossed to and fro, and carried about with every wind of doctrine by the sleight of

men, and cunning craftiness, whereby they
lie in wait to deceive; (Ephesians 4:14).

I am tossed up and down as the locust,
(Psalm 109:23b).

But let him
ask in faith, nothing wavering. For he that
wavereth is like a wave of the sea driven
with the wind and tossed, (James 1:6).

Satan desires to sift mankind like
wheat; sifting implies force against a man,
fragmenting and then scattering.

We pray for our enemy to be
scattered. For the enemy's plans against us to
be scattered. For the power of the enemy to
be scattered, but we must be diligent that we
ourselves are not scattered. We must not be
victims of any *scattering powers*, in the
Name of Jesus. Amen.

Captivity

The enemy has diabolical reasons why he wants to sift or scatter you. Scattering a soul is for a purpose and there is a place where he has for your scattered soul or the parts of it that he has scattered. That part--, those parts are under his auspices if you are captured. You--, or the part of your soul that has been captured is in captivity.

For what I would do, that I do not do. What I would not do, that I find myself doing.

That is the picture of what soul captivity, specifically captivity of the will is. It is incontinence of the will; the person has lost control of their own will. The same will that God allows us to have as free will, when it is captured, Satan is not so generous. He is not generous or merciful at all – he wants your will and works to capture it and put it where he wants it, doing what he wants you to do.

Under his control? Yes. But in hell or other regions of captivity. This is all complicated; do you now see why you need to study your enemy? You need to start as early as possible and always be learning so you will be victorious against him. The devil comes to steal, kill, and destroy, but that doesn't make him a quick study.

To not feel like yourself, to not *be* yourself may mean that your soul or part of your soul is in captivity. Not being able to get your mind off of so and so--, being soul tied is soul captivity. Maybe you can't pinpoint exactly when this started. Maybe it's ever since someone near to you died. Maybe it's ever since you got sick that time. Maybe it's ever since you moved to this particular city, or this particular house. Things just haven't been the same.

Not that it was easy to remember, but perhaps it was ever since you sinned. Ever since you slept with that person who is not your spouse. Ever since you cheated on your exams, ever since you shoplifted. Maybe it wasn't ever since any of those things happened, but shortly after.

I will share that if a person gets a filling on Monday, if that night or Tuesday morning they have a cold or the sniffles, they will swear that the filling or getting the filling *caused* it. Now, if every cause and effect is one hour, two hours, or one or two days away from the event that caused it, I think all humans would be much smarter than they are and much better off. The "punishment" for the sin you may have committed last year may just be showing up, and it's a year later. This could be for any number of reasons. Most often it is because of the prayers of the saints, your repentance, at least partially, and God's abundant Mercy. God has given you time to repent fully and turn from your wicked ways. It didn't take so long to reach you in the physical realm because you got away with it, or because you are so clever, or because God is weak or forgot. It is because of His Mercy toward you.

The incubation period for a common cold is 1 to 3 days. That means that the virus that caused the cold in a person who got a filling on Monday, was in that person's system for that time period before a cold manifested on Monday night. So instead of blaming the dental office, you might want to apologize to them for subjecting *them* to what your body was incubating. Further, a dental office uses all sterilized items on you, wouldn't it make more since that you caught a virus in a non-sanitized, non-disinfected, and non-sterilized place such as the gas station or the grocery store? *Just sayin.'*

The Law is sin, then death. The incubation period for death varies by the person, his sin life, his foundation, lifestyle, and so on; mostly it depends on God's Grace and Mercy. It will be faster for the one God loves and chastises. And, it will be faster for the one who is steeped in sin, knows better but is reprobate; God just takes his hand of protection off that one. It may be slower for one who is called of God and may not even be saved yet. We will see that God is patiently drawing that one.

What's the price of a dental crown? It depends on your dental insurance. What's the iniquity, the **price** of that sin that you committed? It depends on your "insurance", and I don't mean burial insurance, but life insurance. Jesus has already paid the full price for your life, but have you appropriated it? *Have you?*

A curse causeless will not alight. The cause of what anyone is going through today may not have happened yesterday or last night, this is why it is sometimes hard for humans to learn lessons. The lesson may take a long time to get into a person's life, so they may not readily connect the sin to the punishment, or the correct sin to the correct punishment, if there are a lot of sins, but no repentance.

I will scatter them also among the heathen, whom neither they or their fathers have known; and I will send a sword after them, till I have consumed them, (Jeremiah 9:16).

Therefore will I scatter them as the stubble that passeth away by the wind of the wilderness, (Jeremiah 13:24)

Wheat is separated from the chaff by winnowing, which is the blowing of a sustained wind. Job's children suffered that when the building they were all in blew down. Winnowing is a form of threshing, or *sifting*. It was an evil East Wind.

As before stated, it doesn't mean that God *sent* the wind; it does mean that God **allowed** it because of God's own judgment. That punishment came when God passed judgment, or when sin was proved by the Accuser of the Brethren in the Courts of Heaven. Once permission is obtained by the devil, it is now legal against that unrepentant sinner, who keeps sinning. Why? Because he doesn't know, doesn't believe it, doesn't care, and thinks nothing will ever happen to him, so he keeps sinning and doesn't show up to the Courts of Heaven to defend himself.

Sad, because he has the best lawyer, Jesus Christ is our Advocate. He also has the best defense: the Blood of Jesus. It will absolve us of all sin and unrighteousness, but we must show up in the Courts of Heaven and allocute.

The devil is the prince of this world and there are *territorial spirits* operating in regions, the question is posed in Job,

Hast thou commanded the morning since thy days; And caused the dayspring to know his place; That it might take hold of the ends of the earth, That the wicked might be shaken out of it? (Job 38:12)

Random evil may be afoot. If we have not commanded the day, the night, any elements that evil may employ, there may be unexpected damage in a person's life for not being prayed up. As in the natural, those who want to get into a gang must do random violence to "jump" into the gang. Similarly, witches throw out random spells, especially against Christians, just to see if those spells will *hit* anyone. This may be a requirement for them to keep their "powers" or to *jump* into a coven.

My point?

There are evil human agents in the Earth who behave as would-be sifters, shakers, scatterers, and *tossers* 24/7.

Evil Pastors

The evil that is done against people in the Earth is done by other **people**. Some agents know they are doing dark things, others, as we mentioned before may not have any idea that their side hustle is a sin hustle, and they are working for the devil.

Carrying a lot of authority is anyone who calls himself pastor, or operates in that office.

But he that is an hireling, and not the shepherd, whose own the sheep are not, seeth the wolf coming, and leaveth the sheep, and fleeth: and the wolf catcheth them, and scattereth the sheep, (John 10:12)

Besides not looking for the wolves to defend the flock, evil pastors can't see the wolf many times because they **<u>ARE</u>** the wolf.

Live a few minutes, and you will meet all kinds of people. A bad pastor? Yeah, they exist. An evil pastor? Yes, they also exist. There are pastors that lead flocks away instead of finding the lost and gathering them together.

There are so-called pastors who plow with God's heifer. There are pastors who may be deceived or are lost themselves. Whether they started out deceived or became deceived – it doesn't matter; they are deceived. Deceived people deceive people.

Pastors who were never called by God--, but called *themselves* are dangerous and potential scatterers. There are pastors that have been called by flesh, their daddy was a pastor and needed to pass the "business" on to someone in the family.

There are Pastors who've been called by flesh—especially good-looking people, pretty privilege is working *for* that pastor and **against** that congregation, as they have chosen the "leader" that will lead them to their own demise. I heard a woman say that she loved a certain seasoned Pastor and back in the day she and several of her friends went to his church and would follow him anywhere he preached. I was intrigued, so I asked, *Oh, his ministry now, is this what he has always taught, or what did he teach and preach back then?*

She replied, *"I don't know a thing he said, he was just so good looking that I would follow him anywhere he was preaching."*

This is straight up idolatry. She made the preacher into an altar and went to worship him. Whether he or others knew it was not disclosed. She should have been worshipping God, not the mouthpiece. If she thinks she was doing both, she wasn't. If she thought she could get a little tingle for her flesh and a little something for her spirit in one stop, she is wrong. Don't let yourself be led astray just because the speaker is good looking.

Ministers with other gifts and talents are dangerous as well, especially if they are using gifts selfishly. Years ago, I was in love with a certain worship song, so the pastor told me to teach the choir. I was in the choir at that time, so I sat at the piano and began to teach the song. I struck a key, the sopranos sang it beautifully. I gave the next note, the altos chimed in, then the tenors. It was melodious and it was wonderful. However, not for me. I didn't like that level of power over music or the choir. Feeling or knowing I really wasn't called to that, I got up from the piano and never finished teaching that song. Neither God nor any other person told me to sit back down, so I did the right thing.

Satan stole music from Heaven; I don't want any parts of that kind of robbery. There are also music ministers who do all kinds of things with their gifts. Enough said about that.

Woe to those who put up a stumbling block to a seeker. For instance, a beautiful girl wants to be saved, but the person she's asking about the Bible, or about God sees how beautiful she is, and instead wants to date her.

Woe to anyone who leads God's people astray, especially those new in the faith--, the trusting and the vulnerable.

Woe be unto the pastors that destroy and scatter the sheep of my pasture! saith the Lord. (Jeremiah 23:1)

Obviously, those who are scattered from the flock, are easier for the devil to pick off and sift like wheat. They do not enjoy the corporate protection of the congregational fold. In summary, we could say that the scattered have been sifted, or are in the most danger to be sifted. Recall there are many *levels* to the sifting of wheat--, anything from coarse to fine to very fine. If the devil got a hold to anyone, he may not stop at one "sifting."

You, Yourself

The devil wants to sift, toss, thresh, and scatter folks. He would kill them if allowed. If he can't or has another plan for them and their God-given gifts, he will put them, or attempt to put them into captivity. There is such a thing as a captive spirit and a captive soul. The dark world has been known to capture, use, and sell human body parts. (Rev 18:13) – in LIVING people, while they live.

Sounds like something from a horror movie? It is, but it is not just movie lore, because it is also true.

Captive soul means that spiritual captivity has reached the soul.

Captive body means that spiritual captivity has reached the physical body.

It is known in other than Western cultures that a person's *head* is often what is captured first, then the rest will follow. If a mind is captured, the person can be manipulated.

Let's look at the phrases, *And when he had come to himself,* and *Clothed in his right mind.* The person taking the action and the person the action is taken on are one in the same; they are the same person. That may sound weird, but it is essential.

The I AM that I AM – when God said that He is letting all of us know that He is autonomous. Yes, He is Sovereign, but He is in **complete control** of His faculties. I discussed at length in my message, *I Want You Back: Territorial Spirits* and the book that message came from, **What Do You Have to Declare?** how sometimes even your thoughts are not your own, but you think they are, or you are being made to believe they are. When your thoughts are being influenced or controlled by dark forces, your *I am--*, ain't. Whatever is hidden in a soul that is running its mouth gives you thoughts 24 hours a day. Shall you listen?

You shouldn't. But how do you turn it off? How do you get rid of it?

This is why people who "snap", snap. They say they hear voices – and they do…. How do you quiet those voices? You really should, they are planning to lead you astray. They may not be able to get you to go on a crime spree, but then again…

Get rid of them; get deliverance.

When you come to yourself, that's deliverance. When you are yourself, clothed in your right mind at 100% again, that's deliverance.

The Prodigal came to himself… even though in the physical he was captive – yeah, broke, living in a pigpen, desiring to be a servant when he was the son of a man of means --, possibly a king or a prince. The Prodigal was captured in his mind—that's captivity. His *head* has been captured. He's walking around the Earth, no shackles of any kind on him; he's not in a prison, but he is in captivity.

Again, we must open our understanding, we are spirit in a flesh body. What our body does is important, but that is not all there is. What is our spirit doing? Where is our soul and in what condition is that soul?

But a flash of awareness when one comes to himself and asks himself, *What am I doing?* What am I doing *here*? Or in extreme cases, *Why am I with that person? Why am I committing these crimes or sins?* One comes to himself when one comes to a better state, a lucid, coherent state of mind.

When a man is not in his right mind, the nature of demons, devils or idol *gods* has been imposed upon him, and they are doing the thinking for him, although he may think he is doing his own thinking. The emperor's new clothes weren't clothes at all, he was naked. Neither God, nor Jesus, nor the Holy Spirit can lie, so who or what was making the emperor think that he was wearing clothes of any kind, let alone *new* clothes or fine clothes—clothing fit for an emperor or a king?

Demons.

Idol *gods* are always demons. Until deliverance they inhabit the soul of a man; and they talk, talk, talk.

Resisting the devil so he will flee from you is the first line of defense. If you don't do that, then oppression may lead to possession, especially if you are tricked, initiated, rebel, are disobedient, or lukewarm, dry, prayerless, unbelieving--, you're easy to influence.

Once *in*, the sifting can begin from the inside. This can be a double-pronged attack. Know that Satan asks at the Throne of Grace 24/7 to sift you like wheat. What? You thought it was a one-time request? You thought it was only until you got saved?

Contraire, mon frere. It is 24/7.

It is hard to know yourself when your thinking is spirally or squirrelly, this is why we need one another ministry. Listen closely, if you can, when someone in love and in honesty and truth tells you that the way you are thinking, or talking makes no sense; believe them. The idol *gods* (demons) that makes one think or talk a certain way also block their victim's ears, so they cannot really hear themselves, and how ridiculous they may sound. Sin dulls the understanding, so a person's comprehension is diminished. This is why and how a person can be in sin for years and decades; it is a bondage. It is vicious. That soul is scattered, and needs deliverance.

But Jesus restores souls and heals minds; even if sifting, tossing, scattering, or captivity has begun, He can put you back together again. Amen.

When Anything Goes, Anything Comes

Prior to a dental extraction a patient may ask me, *What if my tooth breaks?* I have always told them, *Better that it breaks here, while you're numb, than someplace else.*

How much of a break is too much? Can everything always be put back together again? I've seen dental appliances broken, some can be repaired, some cannot be fixed, but these are manmade things seeking to be repaired by men. I've seen teeth broken; some can be repaired, others, may not be.

God is far greater than anything we have seen and anything we can think of. God can break us in a controlled way, as the clay being broken by the potter, and then put back together properly. There are no pieces too small, there are never too many pieces that God does not know how to reassemble us.

But when we decide to break ourselves, that is by self-destruction, that is the effect of idol *gods* exerting influence upon you. It indicates that they are successful in a third prong of sifting attack. From the outside. From the inside. And now, you, yourself are in self-destruction mode?

We love to say, *No weapon formed –* as said sometimes you help the weapon that will be used against you to form. **Sometimes you <u>ARE</u> the weapon, or the intended weapon, unless you can come to your senses soon enough.**

One of the first signs is when you no longer care. Never say that you don't care, even if you don't, because it invites the most destructive demons into your life and body. When anything goes, anything comes. It comes into your life to steal, kill, and destroy. When we are careless, prayerless, faithless and we allow the enemy to break our spirits or fracture our souls, sifting is the next step.

Humpty Dumpty

Humpty Dumpty sat on a wall.
Humpty Dumpty had a great fall.
All the king's horses and all the king's men
Couldn't put Humpty Dumpty together again.

One of the most shattered things I can think of is Humpty Dumpty; he was in so many pieces that he couldn't be put back together again.

When we can't decide what or who we are, what we should do, when minds are captive and decisions are poor, or non-existent, it's as though we are sitting on a wall. In modern terms, sitting on the fence means one is rather stuck there, not really going one way or the other. It's a risky place. A strong wind (winds of doctrine) blows and you're off that wall, off that fence. Not good! The "wind" of the evil words that the oppressor is speaking inside your head comes, and that will knock you at least off course, but maybe worse. It may take you out, temporarily, or permanently. This is part of the sifting.

Most who are sitting on the fence don't or can't decide and get on with life are as afraid of the future as they are soul tied to the past. The past they think is manageable, because they "know" it--, the future is their unknown.

How, pray tell, might a man move his spirit and body into the future while leaving his soul (mind, will, and intellect) tied to the past. A soul tie is always tied to something in the past, else it would be a lasso that would launch one into their future. A soul tied person, if they talk, will only, or mostly talk of past things.

While a man's soul sits in the past, he is in captivity because there is no place to **park** a soul in the Spirit realm. You couldn't exist without your heart, or your head or other essential body parts. Your soul is essential to your current, daily, successful existence. If you were going through a desert, could you leave your camel back in town and successfully traverse the Sahara, for example? No. Your soul is essential to you, and it works for you, else it would not have been given to you by God. You can't just leave your soul somewhere --, such as in the past, if you are moving forward.

Your soul is of high value, else the devil would not be after it. It is like the carburetor in a car; how far would a car get without a carburetor?

While a man sits in indecision not choosing this side or that side, not choosing forward or backward, there is a third thing that can happen, and that thing is downward – a fall.

Had Humpty, if he were a person with a mind--, had he been more conscious of the fact that downward was a possibility, I'm pretty sure he would have gotten off that fence. Pretty sure I would have, too; how about you? The fall maybe into evil and darkness, the result of a poor choice, no choice, or an evil wind. If we survive the fall, the work can begin. Rock bottom it's called, but it can bring full awareness of the evil that may be working against you to make your life as tough as it is, and as tough as it's been. Rock bottom is full awareness of the evil that may still be operating against your life, health, wealth, education, marriage, children, and success.

Ironic, isn't it. At a high vantage point, you can see so much more than when you're at ground level. But at Rock Bottom, and being able to look up- you suddenly see what you had previously missed. Isn't it amazing what perspective can do?

We need to get off of this threshing floor! Lord, don't let us be threshed, sifted, and/or scattered, in Jesus' Name.

We want out of this pit. NOW! Rock bottom is not at all attractive. It may not be now that we get out of this pit, but as we have mercifully survived the fall, we can now begin the work to get out of it. Our hands will learn to war and our fingers to fight. AMEN!

My Pit

Twenty or more years ago, I was a newlywed. Happy--, of course. One of my favorite weekend activities was the 2pm Sunday nap after church and brunch, and it still is. I would have the best dreams after church.

One Sunday, many years ago, the most horrible dream occurred. What happened in the dream was *too much*, and I didn't even know much about dreams then. Now that I know a bit more about dreams, I know that dream was **super** horrendous.

My husband was nowhere around, but who am I kidding, he'd understand less than I did about this particular dream.

In this dream, which may have been a vision, I was put in a pit.

In this pit (we may say rock bottom) but it was a pit, a well with stone walls, no water but I could see above and daylight. I felt like Joseph may have when he was put in that well with no water in it and was probably befuddled as to why his brothers did this. Was it a gag? Were they coming back? Or panic may have begun to set in, as how could he possibly get out of this place?

In my dream, a man on a white horse came and rescued me. It was as though he reached the entire length to the bottom of this pit with His arm and pulled me out of this pit of captivity. I recall things spinning but I was aware of what was going on in the vision, but I was still asleep.

What was so weird is when I went to sleep, there was a shirt that had been laundered hanging on the bedroom's doorknob, it still had the dry cleaner's plastic over it. Yet, when I woke up it was no longer there, it was on the doorknob of the door of the spare bedroom, down the hall, where no one slept and where no clothes were stored.

I was so thankful to be rescued in the "dream", that I didn't give that shirt that much thought, but no one was home but me so who could have moved it? This let me know that something spiritually deep went on that afternoon.

There are some dreams and visions that are so vivid and important that even years or decades later you remember them clearly. Now that you are who you are in Christ and it's years later, pray and ask the Holy Spirit to interpret what was going on in some of your older, but lucid dreams. That's what I have had to do.

Pull Yourself Together

But if Sir Humpty is an egg, as in the child's rhyme, it is irregular. It can roll and it can wobble, it is not always steady, as it has a round base, not a flat, stable base. It can change directions willy nilly because of its contours, and as stated if a good wind comes along, Humpty can be taken not just off course, but blown away.

When you go through such a dream as being put in a pit, or worse, the little cares of the world seem less important. This is when you start to search to understand what is happening to you in the spirit. That dream was meant to be a trauma, and it could have been a serious trauma, but since I was rescued, it removed the trauma of the dream. So, life goes on. Thank You, Jesus!

I never told anyone about this dream, not my husband, just you readers, all these years later. Since then, I've learned that trauma is a devil tactic, it opens the soul and it fragments and steals parts of the soul.

Saints of God, if it hadn't before, the *threshing, sifting,* and even attempts to bring captivity had begun against me.

Perhaps you can pinpoint a day, hour, event, or even a dream that started your awareness that some tossing, threshing, sifting, or fragmenting had begun against you.

But now we are in Christ, and we are wiser. So we now know that we must put ourselves back together some how. Isn't that what they say in the movies when someone is traumatized, in shock, or going *through?*

Pull yourself together! Pull yourself together, man!

However, even if we are spiritually, soulishly matured, and can easily find center again--, we need Jesus and the Holy Spirit to put ourselves together again. Like Humpty Dumpty, there is no one in the natural, not the king's horses, nor the king's men who can put people back together again, absent God.

Don't try to put yourself together again, alone. This is not a DIY project. If it is a physical break, a surgeon? Yes, but not without God's hand in it. If it is a mental or emotional break, a psychologist or psychiatrist? Most often not--, not without God in it. This is why people can be in "therapy" all their lives and never get fully healed. But that's easy for God; He binds broken hearts, and He restores souls.

Unlike Humpty, in the hands of the king's horses and men, the Lord can put you back together again.

Military Weapon

Behold, I will make thee a new sharp
threshing instrument having teeth; thou shalt
thresh the mountains, and beat them small,
and shalt make the hills as chaff, (Isa 41:15).

The above verse describes threshing
that **you** will do. The script has flipped; the
tables have turned. Once you know who you
are you become the weapon against those
who want to use weapons against you, or
more cleverly, more subtly **make you a
weapon against yourself.**

According to many historians,
Humpty Dumpty was likely a military
cannon in the English Civil War. In 1648
King Charles I had his soldiers (the King's
Men) place several cannons on the walls.
One of these cannons was named Humpty
Dumpty and was placed on the wall of a

church. (And you thought silly nicknames was a modern thing!) *Anyhoo*—Humpty Dumpty fell--, more like got knocked down, knocked out of commission by enemy cannons. Humpty fell off the wall, busted, disgusted--, broken irreparably.

Seems this particular cannon was really needed, because without it in operation, King Charles I lost the battle and the war, ultimately.

Being blown off the wall created the *great fall.*

FYI: According to the Oxford Dictionary, "humpty dumpty" was a 17th century alcoholic beverage. As a result of that, or maybe not, it was also used to describe a short, clumsy person. Note how the first thing an alcoholic drink does is knock one off their own faculties.

This nursery rhyme is a tongue-in-cheek way to indicate that something is beyond repair and cannot be put back together again.

You are a military grade weapon. Well, at least you're supposed to be; you should be a Giant in the spirit.

What wise enemy wouldn't try to **de-weaponize** his opponent? You should be doing that. Anyway, the devil surely is. For those who don't know they are supposed to be a weapon, or don't believe it – life is easy--, until it's not.

So, you're a weapon. Created. Formed. Set on the church wall, on the ramparts. Not just a watchman on the wall, but a watchman with authority and power. But, unless the Lord watch the city, they who watch, watch in vain. Therefore, in Christ you are a strong weapon against evil. Absent God, the power of God, the Holy Spirit, you are not.

In Christ, with the Lord, we can be a strong weapon guarding and protecting the *city*. Sometimes the city is a geographical location. Sometimes, *you* are the city.

You are set in position. Where is that? Wherever the Lord has established that you be. The enemy will fire cannons; he does it all the time. Sometimes cannons may be fired at you; sometimes, as discussed, they are random cannons; pray always not to be in harm's way. You are to stand your ground, guard the wall, watch your territory, and possess your possessions. You are to *occupy* until Jesus returns.

You are not Humpty Dumpty. You are not a loose cannon or a lost, broken, irreparable weapon. You know who you are and you are all put together and **whole**. If someone wants to sift you, you must resist. You must persist in prayer. You are not weaponless, and you are not weak.

Now, w*here are you supposed to be?*

God gives you clues and confirmations, even blessings to assure you of where you are supposed to be.

Grow up. You're not just an egg; an egg was just born yesterday. Grow up in the Lord and things of the Spirit.

Arise and thresh, O daughter of Zion: for I will make thine horn iron, and I will make thy hoofs brass: and thou shalt beat in pieces many people: and I will consecrate their gain unto the Lord, and their substance unto the Lord of the whole earth, (Micah 4:13).

What then, is the solution to all this scattering, shattering, tossing, sifting, and threshing?

We serve both a fierce and a loving God. He is both Creator and a smiter.

He is mighty in battle and does not desire that one of us--, not one of His would be lost.

That then the Lord thy God will turn thy captivity, and have compassion upon thee, and will return and gather thee from all the nations, wither the Lord thy god hath scattered thee, (Deuteronomy 30:3).

Prophetic Word: I have heard the Voice of the Lord saying, I WILL NOT LEAVE YOUR SOUL IN HELL.

If any of thine be driven out unto the outmost parts of heaven, from thence will the Lord thy God gather thee and from thence will he fetch thee: (Deuteronomy 30:4)

For a small moment have I forsaken thee; but with great mercies will I gather thee, (Isaiah 54:7).

Our God is loving, and He is also fierce. As a parent He as to be both, and withholding discipline is not the mark of a good parent.

But I Have Prayed for You

Simon, Simon, Satan has asked to sift all of
you as wheat. But I have prayed for
you, Simon, that your faith may not fail.
And when you have turned back,
strengthen your brothers."

Jesus told Peter, **Satan has asked to
sift you all like wheat.** The fact that Jesus
told Peter that means that was hidden or yet
unrevealed information--, not discerned by
Peter or the Disciples. In addition, Jesus said,
But I have prayed for you; so Jesus had put
the quietus on the devil's request.

*"And when you have turned back,
strengthen your brothers."* That is the
perfect reminder to us that even if we go
through trials and tests in life, once we get
through them, we don't curl up in the corner
or just lay there complaining about all we had
to endure.

Now, we strengthen our brothers.

Jesus said, *But I have prayed for you.* By that time Jesus had been through plenty Himself, yet He still took the time to intercede for those who walked with Him. He interceded for those that He *pastored*, as the Good Shepherd. He prayed for those who were not strong enough or wise enough to pray for themselves. He prayed for those who may not have been spiritually aware as to what was transpiring in Heaven's Courts against them. Jesus said, in response to the devil's request, ask, or demand to have them all and sift them like wheat--, His response was to pray and pray then. Jesus did not wait until after they had been sifting, or even while they were being sifted, but He prayed immediately for them. Jesus also made a finished work of it, else He would have said, I'm *still* praying for you on this matter.

Nope.

He said, *"I have prayed for you."* Indicating that it was done; Jesus finished the matter.

82

Jesus said, *"Greater things you shall do because I go to the Father."* Therefore, we should do as Jesus did and pray for one another, especially if we have a Word that Satan is desiring to sift a brother in the Faith.

Those who know their God shall do exploits.

Been Sifted

If you've been sifted or suspect that you have and no one prayed for you—no one, including yourself because of being undiscerning and/or prayerless, there is work to do.

I had been oppressed by many things for some time. I felt in my spirit multiple altars were emanating against me. A witchcraft altar. Another witchcraft altar. An occultic altar.

Things happen in life, setbacks and disappointments, but we just keep trudging along. After all, the only real option is to press forward. It is not until things get really weird that some of us may consider, *You know this is a deep problem; it might even be a spiritual problem.*

Every problem is a spiritual problem, but is it spiritual **only**, or has this problem transferred or manifested into the physical by the time you notice that it's a problem?

In my late teens, I dated a fellow who, looking back was very *Ahab*-like; he was a nice guy, kinda passive. His mother was his *Jezebel*. She didn't want me to break up with him --, well – I can't prove any of this, but this is my impression of how this may have started, not leaving out my own family's faulty foundation, since no curse can alight without a cause.

Early in my adulthood, there was the witch who worked in the same building with me. She seemed like a nice lady--, so friendly. We are no longer in contact, but it is only looking back with acquired Wisdom that I see that she was/is a witch.

After that, failed relationships and women attached to fellows I'd meet who almost all, without fail, would say, *If you hurt him, I'll do thus and so to you.* Saints, if you've never taken these threats seriously, do. Having a woman say that to you is really odd, because the man is supposed to be protecting the woman, not being cowardly as whether she will "hurt" him or not. Another woman rising up in a masculine spirit to protect *him* is weird; it is not God's order.

Oh, I just realized it –, that was another *Ahab spirit*, and his female friends were his *Jezebels*.

Some years ago – the rat--, that story was shared in another book--, that was either another witch or she was connected to witches, in that she hired them to do things for her. I believe she, herself was a witch.

Some years after that an outright threat was made to my face regarding my business--, but hey, I'm doing everything in my professional life by the book, so there's no way I can get into trouble over anything, was how I was thinking at that time.

I was so engrossed in my professional life I neglected my spiritual life. So, what about my spiritual life? Looking back, I realize the person who threatened me didn't threaten my professional life; she threatened me spiritually, although she didn't say so.

Not that this person had a right to judge me, so I didn't think too much of that.

Saints of God, witchcraft is not done by godly people, and these **UNgodly** people sincerely believe they have a right to blame, try, judge, and execute, if that is their goal. Even if you are doing everything by the book, if you are not prayed up and spiritual-minded, whatever curses they may be slinging may be waiting for an unguarded hour to pounce.

Stay. Prayed. Up.

Then there was the one who turned me over to the tormentors, which I shared at length in my book, **Tormenting Spirits**.

Some years after that a disgruntled unfriendly friend who believes that I caused them to lose their job was most likely the source of some witchcraft sent my way.

Enough altars? You'd think so, but there is at least two more – the old man who blindsided me, from my book, **Blindsided: Has the Old Man Bewitched You?** had started his witchcraft a long time ago, either at the same time as the old woman who worked in the same building as I did early in my career. These two lived in different states and as far as I know did not know each other, but stranger things have happened. The two older folks started their shenanigans at the same time or the man shortly after the woman.

And from my book, **Evil Touch**, another witch, or coven of witches.

There, that's a good collection of witches, witchcraft and covens on my case.

Does yours look anything like this?

Don't panic. It is what it is, and you are the Giant in the Spirit; the Greater One is in you. What is up against you is a huge clue as to who you are to God. Don't look too hard to see *who*, because we won't know who unless the Holy Spirit reveals them to us. As I prayed and prayed--, while praying warfare prayers specifically against witchcraft, for weeks and months, the Spirit showed me face after face, so these things are confirmed by the Spirit.

As stated, you don't need to worry about who, except perhaps to stay clear of them, pray for them if the Lord agrees, and don't go back to the same vomit.

Years have gone by. As most don't believe in witchcraft, I was oblivious and also oblivious that I needed to prayer treat, or **how** to prayer treat anything that was happening in my life in those early years. There was no good Baptist pastor that I could tell any of this stuff to, and even if I did…

Finally, seeking deliverance, in the times of COVID, and finding a bit online, here and there, but not in person, after all the old man was a "pastor." First you have to believe that witchcraft really exists, and it has been used against you --, wrap your own mind around it, then if one of the perpetrators is a *pastor*, who can you trust? This is why deliverance can take so long. You try to do it yourself and you do all you can, pray, praise, worship, study, fast. But when we need help, we need help.

Holy Spirit, you are the Spirit of deliverance. Do a work in me. Amen.

I met a deliverance minister who prayed diligently with me for deliverance on three separate occasions. At the end of that time period, I felt gathered. And that's the why of this book. I didn't even realize that I was scattered and was trying to conduct my life as a scattered person, that is a person with a fragmented or scattered soul.

But I had been threshed, tossed, even sifted, and traumatized, and scattered in life. *Haven't we all?*

After the deliverance, or I should say, after this deliverance that came after at least four or five other deliverances, it was as though my parts had been collected and re-membered – put back together. It was comforting; I felt secure. I felt whole. I felt as if I was one being and hadn't realized that I had been dismantled; I was just trudging on in life.

What Is Old Age?

Sifting doesn't have to be painful. Sometimes you don't even realize that it is happening, or that it happened. Else, you'd do something about it in real time.

The warning here lies in the question, *What is old age?*

Joshua was still strong in his old age; he was not sifted in his youth or earlier in his life.

Apostle John preached to 100 years old – mind good, body strong, not sifted.

People on beds of affliction and sickness, ill, suffering, dying prematurely have most likely been sifted.

Do not wait until your old age to find out if you've been sifted, against your will, against your knowledge and you've done nothing about it for a lifetime and now your years are golden, but your mind and or body may be suffering. It doesn't have to be this way. Psalm 91 says with long life I will satisfy him. There is nothing satisfying about living a long time while sick. God is not a liar; if He said a thing it is true.

Pull yourself together, man! Pull yourself together woman, while you're young, in your middle age and be sure you're all together so as you age, you don't fall apart from the sifting that the enemy has either sprung on you or silently slipped into your life. Get your soul and body out of hock to the devil.

We need Jesus.

- Blood of Jesus buy me back from wherever they have sold me, in the Name of Jesus.
- Holy Spirit gather me from the four corners of the universe and put me back together, in the Name of Jesus.
- Spirit of Deliverance, deliver me; unscatter me, and put my mind, soul,

spirit and body back together; remember me, in the Name of Jesus.

O thou afflicted, tossed with tempest, and not comforted, behold, I will lay thy stones with fair colours, and lay thy foundations with sapphires, (Isaiah 54:11).

Re-Membered: Put Back Together

> For, lo, I will command, and I will sift the house of Israel among all nations, like as corn is sifted in a sieve, yet shall not the least grain fall upon the earth, (Amos 9:9).

God, by His Mercy, will chastise, punish, teach, and then draw us back to Him. By the time we take punishment and learn our lesson, we should be running back to God, then He will receive us.

Why? Because we've dropped those *idols*, those idol *gods* and are serving the One True God, only.

Before, when we served other *gods*, either consciously or unconsciously, we were not pleasing to, or attractive to God. Before, when we served other *gods*, and even though those idols worked for Satan, the devil would and still could go to the Courts of Heaven and accuse us of idolatry, and if we did not defend ourselves with Jesus Christ as our Advocate and the Blood of Jesus as our defense, the devil could get a judgment against a man to *sift him like wheat.*

Now that we are saved and delivered, or at least *seeking* deliverance, we are filling up more and more with the Holy Spirit, as well in Christ, when God looks at us, He sees Christ, not us in our own polluted blood. When God looks at us, He is not bound by Time or space, so He sees the future us--, the one that is fully delivered, saved, set free, set aside and fully in Christ.

Who remembered us in our low estate: For his mercy endureth for ever:

And hath redeemed us from our enemies: For his mercy endureth for ever.

Who giveth food to all flesh: For his mercy endureth for ever.

O give thanks unto the God of heaven: For his mercy endureth for ever.

(Psalm 136:23-26) **Amen.**

Dear Reader

Thank you for acquiring and reading this book. I pray that it has enlightened and strengthened you.

May the Lord break you out of every captivity. May He gather you in all places that you have been scattered.

And may He restore you *at least* sevenfold, all that you have lost and all that has been taken from you. Even *time,* as He restores the years. In the Name of Jesus, Amen.

Dr. Marlene Miles

Other books by this author

AK: The Adventures of the Agape Kid

AMONG SOME THIEVES

Ancestral Powers

Blindsided: *Has the Old Man Bewitched You?*

https://a.co/d/5O2fLLR

Churchzilla, The Wanna-Be, Supposed-to-be Bride of Christ

Demons Hate Questions

Devil Weapons: Unforgiveness, Bitterness,...

Dream Defilement

Don't Refuse Me, Lord (4 book series)

Every Evil Bird

Evil Touch

Fantasy Spirit Spouse

FAT Demons (The): *Breaking Demonic Curses*

The Fold (4 book series)

The Fold (Book 1)

 Name Your Seed (Book 2)

The Poor Attitudes of Money (3)

Do Not Orphan Your Seed

got HEALING? Verses for Life

got LOVE? Verses for Life

got HOPE? Verses for Life

got money?

How to Dental Assist

How to Dental Assit2: Be Productive, Not Wasteful

Let Me Have A Dollar's Worth

Living for the NOW of God

Lose My Location https://a.co/d/crD6mV9

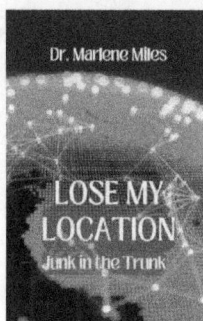

Man Safari, *The*

Marriage Ed. Rules of Engagement & Marriage

Made Perfect in Love

Motherboard (The)- soul prosperity series

Plantation Souls

Power Money: Nine Times the Tithe

The Power of Wealth *(forthcoming)*

Rules of Engagement & Marriage

Seasons of Grief

Seasons of War

Sift You Like Wheat

Soul Prosperity soul prosperity series 3

https://a.co/d/5p8YvCN

Souls Captivity soul prosperity series 2

The Spirit of Poverty

This Is NOT That: How to Keep Demons from Coming At You

Throne of Grace: Courtroom Prayer

Time Is of the Essence

Too Many Wives: *Why You Have Lady Problems*

Tormenting Spirits   https://a.co/d/dAogEJf

Triangular Power *(series)*

>Powers Above

>SUNBLOCK

>Do Not Swear by the Moon

>STARSTRUCK

Uncontested Doom

Upgrade: How to Get Out of Survival Mode

Toxic Souls (Book 2 of series)

Legacy (Book 3 of series)

Warfare Prayer Against Beauty Curses

Warfare Prayer Against Poverty

What Have You to Declare?

When the Devourer is Rebuked

The Wilderness Romance *(series)*

- *The Social Wilderness*
- *The Sexual Wilderness*
- *The Spiritual Wilderness*

www.ingramcontent.com/pod-product-compliance
Lightning Source LLC
LaVergne TN
LVHW051424080426
835508LV00022B/3228